Like her beautiful first *Etude for Belonging* manag— — —.....p.. ....u .uuu.uuu ai uic same time, hiding breathtaking and often daring choices in the spaces between words or lines, like a seamstress using solid gold thread on interior hems. I encourage readers to consider reading this book aloud to a loved one. There's so much to take from these poems; it's a joy to share the treasure you'll discover with someone who may need it even more than you do.

Benjamin Gorman
author of *The Sum of Our Gods* and *Don't Read This Book*

Bethany Lee's *Etude for Belonging* gives me hope at a time when it is most needed. Like the trees about which she writes in "Reaching Out," each poem in this new collection offers profound connection to Lee and to the world she inhabits. I'm grateful for the sense of loving acceptance and community Lee crafts through her beautiful words—words that convey to the reader that "We can stand together." That sense of unity, of belonging, is a gift.

Melanie Springer Mock
professor at George Fox University and author of
Worthy: Finding Yourself in a World Expecting Someone Else

Bethany has done it again! This book is "the blessing / of a room where strangers sit / breathing unashamed / into a chosen silence." Bethany is a curator of quiet spaces. She gently points us to the center, to "the swirling heart that binds us / all in place," and whispers, "This could be the better." Even if "there may come all I fear / and several horrible things I failed to consider," this is a book to soothe and inspire.

Joann Renee Boswell
author of *Cosmic Pockets*,
poetry editor for Untold Volumes, skeptical mystic

Vital, beautiful questions spin like planets in Bethany Lee's *Etude for Belonging*, circling around the miraculous sun of love. As readers, we are spun lovingly with her as she asks, "What does it cost to fall in love with the world?" The answer is joyously seeded throughout poems which are generous and knowing in the tradition of Hafez and Rumi and other poets of the world and soul. This is a welcoming book, a book of *Yes* that makes room for us all. It is a necessary answer to pain and destruction. May it carry, astonish, and change you.

Annie Lighthart
author of *Pax*, *Iron String*, and *Lantern*

There are promises here such as, "There is wholeness in the heart of things / and you are in the heart of the heart." There are unexpected questions and loving answers. Bethany offers us a world that is real in the pain and grief, and alluring in the possibility of available beauty. She invites you to "stand near a window and sing in the mystery." Don't resist! Stand by this window. "As you wait / there will be transformation."

Peg Edera
author of *Love is Deeper than Distance: Poems of love, death, a little sex, ALS, dementia, and the widow's life thereafter*

Bethany will take your hand, gently beckoning, "You're not doing courage wrong, if it doesn't feel brave." She'll ask you to stop and look at the stars, giving you enough space to let your sighs slip from your body. Then, when you are quiet enough to feel the heartbeat of the world, she'll whisper in your ear, "How long can you suspend your disbelief?" Follow the notes of her song, dance together on the shoreline of creation, and don't be afraid to join in on the chorus. Sing the song of being alive.

juniper klatt
author of *I was raised in a house of water* and *I wrote this naked*

Bethany Lee's poems speak plainly of the storms, pain, and hungers of daily life, offering a profound hope for transformation. Even so, "Hope is manual labor," she writes. "Get right in there and mix up a batch." These tender poems accompany the reader as they turn to this work, offering the language of nature, Spirit, and a radical acceptance of the reader themselves.

Jennifer L. Hollis
music-thanatologist, writer,
and the author of *Music at the End of Life:
Easing the Pain and Preparing the Passage*

Etude for Belonging

Poems for Practicing Courage and Hope

Bethany Lee

Fernwood
PRESS

Etude for Belonging

Poems for Practicing Courage and Hope

©2021 by Bethany Lee

Fernwood Press
Newberg, Oregon
www.fernwoodpress.com

Printed in the United States of America

Cover and page design: Mareesa Fawver Moss

Cover photo: Kesia Lee

Author photo: Bec Joy España

ISBN 978-1-59498-075-6

Poems previously published in *Untold Volumes* (Christian Feminism Today):

Redeliverance (January 2020)
From Under the Air (July 2020)
To Mend Them (December 2020)

Poems previously published in *What Canst Thou Say* (August 2020):

Compline
Coda

For Jenn and Tamarah, who see and love
the earliest drafts of my words and my heart.
And for you, who are reading this one.

Contents

Introduction

When you open this book, it will be like you have just found it in a room for meditation or left outside in the shade of an old tree or on the kitchen table of a reliable friend: something both familiar and strange in the incantations' beckoning.

As a musician who plays harp for hospice, Bethany Lee lives at the boundary between great beauty and the dark, and from that periphery as a poet, she brings forth spells to kindle spirit and calm the heart. You will find in this book poems for all seasons of a day and chapters of a life. In the foreground, she gives us the trouble, beauty, and enigma of this life, and each poem is a threshold reaching for "what's on the other side."

Many of these poems become a kind of crucible into which are gathered sensations, mysteries, provisional landmarks, beauties, and pangs of trouble, and by the end of the page, they've all been transformed into an elixir for calm.

I often feel at that point on the page, I've been gifted with a tune.

Just as evening comes to benedict each day, the dusk-hinge that closes away to-do and leaves you ready for rest, these incantations put away your troubles in a drawer and invite you to light a candle of awareness.

These poems practice "the knack / of seeing the essence," which is something we need in this world of propaganda for false riches. Behind commerce, beyond striving, on a different path than ambition, moments of waking keep appearing in this book like sunlit arenas in a dark wood or a dream that lifts you out of sleep or a blossoming strike of notes on the harp.

Kim Stafford,
author of *Singer Come from Afar*

Acknowledgments

Deep gratitude

to Mom, Dad, Mauri, Kieran, Evgeny, Erin, Kyle, Betty, Jill,
    Kim, and John
music teachers and inspirations,
who taught me etudes for my fingers and practices for life

to Eric and Mareesa from Fernwood Press, who pinned this
    collection to the page,
making it stronger and more beautiful along the way

to the people of West Hills Friends for your wholehearted embrace
and for being a place where silence blooms

to the gathering affectionately called Church with Cats,
especially Leslie, Rebecca, and Katie, for making room for the
    currents to flow
(and to the cats, for joy)

to Polly, Peggy, Lisa, Jennifer, Ben, Peg, Juniper,
Brett, Melanie, Howard, Ellen, and many more—
constellation of writers that keeps me shining

to Kim, who listens and makes room for others to do the same

to Jo, who fills a space I didn't know was empty

to Kate, who carries me

to Hannah and Meira, my galaxy

to Bryan, far beyond words

and finally, to my own courageous soul for braving the becoming
and writing about it

Wonder

Does it ever stop being amazing?
I plan to never stop being amazed

Begin Here

Could I have noticed the falling leaves
through the window of my own room?

Cherished the way
the woods smell in the fall—
musk of bark and crimson's decay?
Fallen in love all over again
under my own gray sky?

Could I have given my body
the gift of this pleasant day
untied the knots
binding soul to racing mind
and let each thought float
free as a gull
from the ground I walk every day?

I could, yes
yes
but afraid I would not
I came away
to the place with the secret door
I have never once found locked

How do you slip through?

Daily Offering

If all of it is burning
in the kindled flame of life
and time itself is blazing
future's fuel to yesterday's ash

If it's all going up in smoke
today's tasks remaining
not a cosmic moment
more or less
than redwoods
cathedrals
constellations

all I can do is decide
what to feed the fire
choose my incense wisely
burn beauty

Harmonic Phenomenon

Earth makes a tiny seismic rumble every 26 seconds.
Is the pulsating caused by ocean waves, volcanoes,
or something else completely? Theories abound.
The "microseism" doesn't seem to be hurting anything
and has not been a high priority.

   —Caroline Delbert

"But what makes the magnet work?" I asked
and the teacher gave an answer
"It has a positive and a negative, see?
And opposite poles attract, see?"

I saw. But I didn't know why
she wouldn't tell me how
and I didn't yet recognize
the specific set of the mouth
when someone doesn't want
to have to say, "I don't know."

It takes singing whales years
to get bored of their latest hits
start working on a new piece
and pass around the tune
If you stick your head underwater
at just the right time
hold your breath and pay attention
you can hear the hallelujahs

How many more of us
would have ended up scientists
if our teachers had stopped passing out
answers and started serving up
questions instead?

The humpbacks on the west
coast of Ghana have been dying
and no one knows for sure why
The earth nearby thrums with a beat
that no one understands
One hundred and fifty times an hour
Steady as a pounding heart

For years the whales sang in time
with the long-tempoed pulse
I have heard them in the night
the drums of my own ears
throbbing to their chorus

but the noisy search
for crude black gold
has silenced the vital song
Maybe whales know
even better than we do
you can live without gold
but not without singing

Cultivate

Since it is spring
and the ground is ready
we are planting seeds
trusting the turning earth
to bring the harvest

Choosing carefully
the fruit we will need
preserved for winter days

We have been practicing
for a long time now
planting in our own soil
the seeds of our own harvest

Even the roots of what
you thought were weeds
can save your life

Reaching Out

Do the trees know the people are suffering?
Do they hear the cries
of those who are dying alone
and those who are mourning in isolation?

They would have every right
to turn away from our anguish
we who have not been heeding theirs
even as the fires burned
and commerce slashed the earth

Is the sight of the clear blue sky
more beautiful than the flight
uniting loved ones from afar?

Do they hear the silent streets
more loudly than our weeping?

I cannot believe it to be true
for this is not the way of trees
who carry what they need
in the ground they share
pass it along freely
to the weary ones among them

Why should we not think
they wish to do the same for us?
Why should we not believe
they wish for us to do the same?

They are reaching out their limbs to say
This is the way for us all to grow
They are calling with their quiet roots
We can stand together

To Enter the Mystery

I wish for you the blessing
of a room where strangers sit
breathing unashamed
into a chosen silence

Not the gasping breath
of travelers on a crowded plane
or the tenuous wheeze
of the waiting room

May you know the power
of those who have decided
to submit to the silence
to enter the mystery
be consumed by it
and emerge transformed

May you belong among those
who inhale the stillness
as if it is keeping us
because it is
keeping us alive

Collected in the Quiet

At the Maplewood Meetinghouse

I don't know how we even stand up
(there can be joy in the falling)
I'm already in the process of finding out
what's on the other side

Sit and rest for a moment—
there it is
a necessity of things that amount to practice

There always is something that saves me—
it isn't just me, you know
but something larger than the whole—
I don't know a better word for it than *Spirit*

For the Meek

Who must die for the meek to inherit the earth?
I would love to meet the one
who has made the gentle their successor
And what if this is why
the ones who think they own the earth
are killing the meek to keep it?
But what if the earth inherits herself
keeps writing up wills on every autumn leaf
and announcing herself the beneficiary
every blooming spring?
What if she has placed her whole estate
in escrow for tomorrow
banked away inside the thin skin of the onion bulbs
and under the oak tree in the acorn's shell?
What if she hides herself so she can find herself in winter?
What if she gives herself away
so there is no need to kill over her abundance
only to wait, which we are not very good at
and to trust, which frightens even the bravest soul?
And here, you are asking me
Wait for what? Trust in whom?
But it is not me you should be questioning
Have you tried seeking the green?
Have you considered listening to the soil?

Incantation

Write your questions down
Fold them up and put them in your pocket
Forget about them and go for a walk

Wash your pants
until your enigma
turns liquid
until the water
and the motion
felt the fibers
soften the mystery

Go to a place where you can be alone
for a while
where you can be
for a while

Reach inside and hold your wondering
Close your eyes
Say the magic words
(only you know what they are)
Mine usually sound like *thank you*

Find something to wave
a piece of ribbon
a friendly hand
a tuneful breath
the sea

Wield your wand
and wait

I'm sorry to say
you will not get an answer
(Did you think that's what the mages do?)

Your fear will not vanish
your hope not appear
but as you wait
there will be a transformation

Sacrament

I took my soul down to the river today
pulled it out and knelt down
on a pebbled bank at a quiet turn

It was travel-worn and a little grimy
but I held it in my hands
without judgment or rejection

I lowered it into the water
opened my grasp to the flow
and waited for the cleansing
for the revelation

Course Made Good: 315° True

My dentist says she can tell
that I brush my teeth top to bottom
starting in the upper left
"I can see the place you're worn away."

At the gallery, I look up first
up and left after a lifetime trained
by the vagaries of written words
Where would Socrates have looked
and where Homer, his mind a nautilus
of epic and memory?

The first time I slid into the seat to the right
my daughter behind the wheel
I reached up and left
to the center for my seatbelt

One day my children began showing up
in new shoes, in clothes I didn't shop for
with thoughts I didn't give them
Your fear didn't stop me from rejoicing

On the map I was raised with
the northwest is on top, always to the left,
the first place I begin and return
But the earth is round
I hold it in my hands in every orientation
let it string out into the silent wild sky

You weren't given the chance to be yourself
so you don't know what to do when I take mine
take my own chances
own my own existence
roll it around in my palms
find the thread and let the world go

Inside a maze there is no top
you can turn it over in your mind
looking forever for what is left

What do I bury for my children
and how do I draw the treasure map?
Weapons for war, soles for walking
Will I recognize the birthright
once it slips onto their feet?

Instead of a rusty inherited sword
and mouldering sandals,
fashioned for use, out of fashion now,
what if I plant instructions for making—
how to forge your own protection
and weave what you need
to walk freely in the world?

Look up, look at what I've left
Don't dwell there too long
or you'll wear a hole in your life

The crescent moon hangs high,
is left in the sky only after the sun has set
and it is finally
dark enough to shine

Uncharted

If I had the choice
would I pay the price?
The life I have now
for the one I lost to get here?

I doubt I would have braved the trade
if offered the exchange

For the sea one must sail
from one life to the other
is treacherous and deadly
and no one makes it across unmarred

Shipwrecked, though—set adrift
only one choice was given
to row against the tide
toward a shattered shore
or to set out through the storm
on an uncharted course
with faith the world is round
and the stars to guide us home

Praise Song for Boatmates

Some of them were brought here
without knowing why
and not everyone has their sea legs
but here we are, crewing
this ramshackle life
over to the other shore

Praise for the one
who brings laughter
on the coldest night watch

Praise for the one
who knows the way
even in the fog
can smell the land
and steer clear until
approaching safe harbor

Praise the one
who teaches the others
to make the sails fast
and the one who sits at the bow
and mends

Praise for those strong enough
to weigh the anchor
and praise for the one
brave enough to away

Praise the cargo keepers,
the galley watch,
those steady enough to walk
the passageways beneath the surface

Praise the one in the crow's nest, who,
though her eyes have never seen it
is always expecting
at any moment
a new world

Singularity

I was a star once
I was the sun at the center
and small bodies found
their orbit around me

We were made of light
and we sailed through space
a matter of nuclear
indivisibility

A form this massive
drawn this tightly
was bound to go supernova
Let it all fly

And when it did
some days were nebulous
thick clouds surrounding
the melding particles

Some days I wondered
if we'd all fall in
to the black hole forming
where once light had been

One day I looked around
at what had coalesced
expanded and contracted
commenced a revolution

Rhythm shifted elliptically
Apogee and perigee
and sometimes,
unpredictably, syzygy

My whirling trembled
at the loosening forces
My circuit arced
tilted, held

Once I was a star at the center
I was the sun
Now all flame, all fly
We have become a galaxy

Walking on a Crowded Path

One man stops
just ahead
leans in close
and investigates
the cedar's upright bark

The twins' mother apologizes
as she eases the stroller past
How can I say
I am glad to make space
for you
for you all?

My judgments
for the man unaware of his vulgar voice
the overdressed girls in furs and heels
the ones who don't seem to be paying attention
(at least not to the same things as me)
float up iridescent
fill with laughter
and dissolve

I too am getting in the way
I too am spoiling the view

At every turn an interruption
and invitation
that brings me back to where we are
which is here
which is together

For When We Are Together

I was going to give you
a poem about cooperation or
rather not *about* cooperation
so much as pointing toward it
as one would point to
the birds building a nest
in spring with reverence and
giddy delight and stillness
but without staring too much
into their eyes

I thought about the piece
from that little green book
with the lines about sharing
bread and making tea for your enemy
but then I remembered
I had loaned it to Carol who
must have needed it more
than I did because
she kept it or maybe she
passed it along to someone she knew
who needed to be reminded
how to hope

So I sat on the floor
in front of my bookshelf
and read a little
Hafez and a little William Stafford
and got in everyone's way
and only found what I wasn't looking for

If I'd come to your house
we could have read
your favorites instead
and we could have pointed out
beauty to each other as a remedy
for what is killing our world
and at some point it is almost certain
you would have put out a bowl of nuts
or an orange perfectly sectioned
and then you would have had
to turn the pages for me
after my fingertips grew sticky
from the sweetness

and I would have picked
the meat from the shells
and placed it broken and shining
in a bowl you bought from the potter
at last year's market
who always got her clay
from the place by the ocean
and finished her work
in someone else's fire

and if we had looked out the window
we would have seen a fresh-laid egg

Center

Fear lives in the top of the hourglass, counting down
the running grains to the last
full moon, holiday,
heartbeat,
kiss

Regret
lives at the bottom
of the heap beneath the mountain
of gold, buried under that which has already fallen

Life chooses the flow

Attend

Art is what you make
with what you notice
It is attention embodied

Let us attend to what we love

Impulse

I didn't have a desert handy
to follow in the footsteps
of Moses and the mystics

So I began to learn to walk on water
against the flood at the river's mouth
into the salt and wild

If the surface of the water
is where the Spirit moves
that's where I want to be, too
out where the sea is always
turning into sky

If you go
if you stay there long enough
the things of the deep may break through
reveal themselves for a moment
before returning to the source

I cannot remain in company
with wonders from beneath
caught as I am
in the air below the stars

But I want to be in attendance
when they rise

For Courage and for Light

What if you went on a pilgrimage
to the home of the one
who changed your life?
Would it be your mother's
Neruda's or Mendelssohn's?
The man on the side of the road
or your third grade teacher
whose words still have a place
on the bookshelf of your heart?

Would your journey take you
through Muir Woods
where the redwoods wear
the tallest crowns
or past the stacks in the library
where you were first cracked
an egg hatched open
on the surface of L'Engle
Harper Lee and Le Guin
(and that's just the L section)?

What offering would you take
to pay your respects
and how would you bow in homage?
What do you bring to give thanks
for courage and for light?

What if when you arrived at the home
and reached to open the door
of the one who changed your life
what if you discovered it was your own?

Grand Unification Theory

. . . the world is a continuous, restless swarming of things,
a continuous coming to light and disappearance of ephemeral entities. . . .
A world of happenings, not of things.

—Carlo Rovelli
from *Seven Brief Lessons on Physics*

A hundred years past Heisenberg
and we still don't understand
how the quanta be
only how they are
as they relate
to each other

This peanut shell just fell
from the breeze into my lap
I cannot know what force
carried me across its path

And you?
How is it that you and I
have come together this way
here in this marvelous entanglement system?

The constant is this:
if you look
you will be
constantly
surprised

I am blown away

Spellbound

The trick is to see people
past all the forms
our masks of fear can take

Practice on dear friends
and small babies and complete strangers
Then move on to those who confuse
irritate, or oppose you

Once you have the knack
of seeing the essence
at the center of it all
you must only remember to do so
and suddenly
at every moment
the world is filled with light

Altered

There is only a trickle
where once there was a river
Somewhere upstream
a landslide blocked the flow
The terrain irrevocably altered

I want to attend to this channel
as carefully as the river
though it ripples through culverts
and roadside ditches
not nearly the splendor
I had once thought possible

But thirsty deer still come
to the edges to drink
and up in the mountains
for those who will follow the stream
and climb past the wreckage
there is a still, deep lake
reflecting the sky

Good Currency

In exchange for rent
a garden tended

A dozen eggs
in thanks for poetry

A song freely offered
refills the channels

When left undammed
the currents flow

Serenade

For the musicians at St Vincent hospital

With these keys
we unlock the door
to a place with rooms
for everyone
We pound the hammers
and build the space
where all can enter
and be blessed
There is rest here
even for the passerby
even for the one most restless
We throw notes
out the windows extravagantly
They fall like blossoms
onto bent heads below
float over the ones carrying heavy burdens
and the ones who bow to share the load
The notes drift down
Each finds a home
The people stoop to pick them up
and are themselves uplifted
Every leaf is scored with beauty
with hope
with peace
with grace

Alchemist

She is turning candlewicks and ink
to beauty
Bird song and silence
and a blue mug of tea
shaded gardens and sea swell
transform before her eyes
to a ribbon of poetry
a newborn line
of delicate harmony
Fresh picked berries
the love of dear friends
pain and grief and laughter
and the weight of
one
cat's
paw
in the morning grass
Stir
wait
watch
Wave the pen like a wand
and breathe
three
deep
breaths
toward the place
where surprise abides
Watch
just there
at the center
Fire

Meantime

When traveling at sea
I learned not to wait
for the passage to end
to pay attention

as if I could press pause
on my being
until I reached my destination

Stay awake
Watch for beauty
Care

This is our life for now
This is our life, now
as it has always been
Now is life is now

On the Bench in Front of the Library at 11:45

They extended the hours for Tuesday
and Thursday evenings
but the tradeoff is the late
opening on Friday

The sun is out though
and the March air finally
feels hopeful

Some are here just for the cloud
of wireless internet that
hovers around the Carnegie bricks

There, mother and daughter are waiting
to go in, though I don't know what
they will do with the dog
when they do. He may wait
by the bike rack

I can see the flag
at the post office across the way
lifting away from the pole
just a bit in the breeze

And across the street
in the tree where at Christmas
the fire department used to hang lights
the birds are making mad love
and singing

Underfoot the paving stones
bear the names of those who gave
or of those who were honored
for all they had already given

Now they are arriving in earnest
"Oh, I didn't think to check the hours!"
(The book return is always open)
"It's five till; we don't have long to wait."

And out on the corner
by the wild rose bushes
the peace pole stands, proclaiming
Que la paz prevalezca en la tierra
May peace prevail on the earth

Today the Leaves Are Turning

If I want
can I turn with them?

If I sit long enough
for the trees to change
will something in me
unloose, release
fall and be set free?

The revolution
spins away
what no longer
sustains

Stillness calls my soul
to alight

Turning to Tears

"What if someday," she said, "we look back
and *these* are the good old days?"

And we were all weeping already
if not aloud then with our bones
turning to tears within us
turning to fire, to fear, and ashes

And there was soap making and sourdough
and questions of matter
and wondering if any of it did

And yet, I had stood where she was standing
on the rise of perspective
where the air is just clear enough
to find your way to wonder
to let something fall away

But I held on with faltering hands
to all I hoped would return

Compline

I try
every evening
to pay attention
but often by dusk
I have been distracted by the day
by the rush of homecoming
or the heading out for hurried plans

I may be too busy noticing
the wear in the mat by the door
or the onions browning
in the heavy red pot
on the unwashed stove

But at twilight
whether I know it or not
I trip over a point
that restores my balance

This is the great and daily evening
where just for a moment
everything comes to level again

Light and dark
sound and silence
work and rest
effort and surrender

If I am very still
will I notice the pause
like the breath at the top
before the wild descent?

Rest easy
Tomorrow there will be
an evening again

A Promising

I pledge allegiance to lunation
and to the citizens who live
in the sway of her light

We are lunatics all
mad with silver-hearted beauty

To the crystalline moment
just after sunset
and the burgeoning fullness
watching over the night

To the fading oval
that shines with the joy
of passing on into darkness

And to new moon's day
when we receive again
the gift of believing
what we cannot see

Missive

I need to go today
to say goodbye to the ocean

Although you never know
each time you turn away
from the one you love
which will be the last

Sometimes you suspect
and sometimes you know—
it could be a long time

Will she send me tidings
through her friends, the stars?
Will the moon, her playmate
bring me news from afar?

And what will the sea say to me
after all the nights we spent together?

Haphazard Masonry

Just because I haven't always
taken the time to wonder
over each egg I crack
and sifted cup of flour

Just because I have sometimes—
often—flung my thanks
carelessly toward the hands
extending what I need

And just because I know
I will someday fail again
to maintain this marveling
as the seasons pass

doesn't mean I am wrong
to tend today with this much care

For each moment
I can bear to live this awake
adds a trace to every one
that has come before

Today's attention
will be tomorrow's altar

Heal

After you give up all the other options
love comes easy

The Gathering

You can't always see a storm coming
but at some point it arrives
a hint on the horizon
a change in the pressure
the wind rising
and rising again

You don't want to wait too long
to shorten your sails
You get down and stay low
You do what you have to do
to get through
You do what you can
to stay kind

The storm doesn't come
carrying a schedule
"I'll be gone by morning"
and once you're in the dark
you can't tell where the cloud bank ends
and where the light begins

At some point you will have done
everything there is to do
and the only thing left
is to wait the wind out
let the waves roll over
shudder to the surface again

It's an uncertain
underwater journey
You're not doing courage wrong
if it doesn't feel brave

Into the Depths

As a child I never dove
in all at once
Most of my life was spent on tiptoe
edging deeper into murky water
while others did cannonballs
and handstands
Because there were small
pinchy monsters in the deeps
and I recoiled from the cold
choosing rather the long
slow suffering of submerging
one scant inch at a time
so only a thin band—
first around my calves,
then my knees, my thighs
my hips and waist—
could feel the pain
All beneath was numb
All above held lifted away
I had to become willing
to give in to the depths
risk the monsters and the pain
I had to become able to bear the truth
underneath the surface of it all
dark and cold
and fertile with silt and movement

Heartwood Is Made from What Has Died

When I came to you
with my soul in my hands
opened them to show you the seed
I was beginning to sense it held
and asked if you thought
it might grow into a tree

You said no
that my seed was not
the right kind of seed
that it was too big
and too small
that it was not a seed at all

You said it hurts to sprout
that there is no more room
in the forest where you stand
that trees just get cut down anyway

And though I believed you for a while
I kept one hand on my heart
where the husk lay broken open
and you were right about one thing—
it hurts to sprout

But now that there is a sapling
roots firmly planted in her mother
and the promise of fruit and shade
at the edge of the branches
it feels almost safe to say
what I never wanted to be true

To live and die a tree
I had to turn away from you

Torn

I.
The altar will be filled

I am waiting
for time to turn symbol
into sacrament

There must be an emptiness
a receiving allowing

this fullness, like a flood
like fragrance rising
from the shattering

In time
the altar will be filled
I am waiting

II.
The altar will be filled
I am waiting

for time to turn symbol
into sacrament
There must be an emptiness

a receiving allowing
this fullness, like a flood
like fragrance rising

from the shattering
In time
the altar will be filled

I am waiting

After the Burning

We never find out what they were called
Job's ten lost children
All we get are some of the names
of the replacement set
in a rare moment in history
when the girls are acknowledged
and the men are anonymous
Jemimah
Keziah
Keren-happuch
It is said they were very beautiful
as if that makes it okay
the others were still dead

And what of that I cannot bear to name
this loss I cannot relinquish?
I refuse to set it down
must not let it rest
or I may be faced
with who I have become
now that I am mostly whole

How can I carry on
into a land where there is not
even a scrap
of what would have been
to comfort me?

It is a cold journey
through that desert
to where I may someday dwell
and many nights I would turn back
if I was not, with each step
setting the land aflame

That day in the church
I was given the choice
to attend to the loss
or turn toward joy
Having had enough of pain's company
I chose to look joy straight in the face
and in that moment
every feature was the twin of grief's

I think I finally understand
why they free climb El Capitan
why the base jumpers
throw themselves from the brink
There at the edge
are grief and joy together
There in the falling
is being alive and knowing it

What Remains

At the bend in the road
where I turn to the left
there was once a giant oak
tall trunk and rounded crown
epitome of tree

One day, years ago now
I rounded the corner and gasped
The perpetual tree had split in two
Half stood mangled, wounded
sap oozing from the rend
Half lay in pieces on the ground

Over the next few months
I looked for the tree every time I drove by
Watched as the fallen fragments
were scattered, removed, decayed

The next year, the remainder fell too
and I mourned both losses
grieved anew at the absence
every single time I passed
seeing only what was no longer there
heedless of that which grew in its place

Today I looked past the ghost of the tree
toward the field and the hills beyond
For the first time in a long time
I could see the sky

Poetry Is Saving My Life Right Now

Oh, please. Don't hear this as the lofty ideal
of a disconnected one, hovering, toes recoiling
over the humble, sacred ground
This is me, tempted to doomscroll all day long
alternating between glee and guilt at the sense
that the long awaited uppance has got up and come
only frightened for where the shrapnel will hit me
or the ones I love, which, I remember now
is everyone, is all of us. No man is an island
no matter how one has tried to float
alone and there is no joy in bad news
but I would forget this if not for the day
I had already dedicated to poetry
and wasn't it Annie Dillard who said
that how we spend our days is,
of course, how we spend our lives?
So when I say that poetry is saving
my life right now, I only mean that *now*
and *now* and *now* with the aid of these words
I am moving again toward the beauty
and my life, the unwieldy brief
bit of time and matter I carry with me
is coming along

Reduction

We didn't have to practice
the truest abundance
when the shelves were always full
of strawberries in December

But we have been reduced
to daily bread from pantry bins
reduced, I think, as a sauce is reduced
as it concentrates to essence
deepens with time
becomes richer from the flame

Enough is far less than we might think
Enough is far more than we might fear

Listen to the ones
who have lived for long with less
They will lead us all to plenty

From Under the Air

When you weep
and grow weary
of the pain
in this world you made
and tire of the weight
of all who cry out
and gasp at the ways
that fear unsettles the souls
uproots those planted in you
tosses them to the winds in terror
where do you take refuge?

Do you sink into the deepest pool?
Find your way along the rising thread
to the heat at the center
the swirling heart that binds us
all in place?
Do you let yourself be held
by the gravity?

Or do you find a home
among the leaping ones?
The rays who bound
from sea to sky?
The orca launching high
from under the air?

Yet even there is no escape from grief
Witness the mother who carried
her lifeless calf
for seventeen days
and
seventeen
nights

A howling protest
or proof of the strength
of mothers who have the will
to carry loss
far beyond a heart's bearing

You, Mother of us all
how long
have you been carrying us on your fin?
Do you, too, grow thin
waiting for resurrection?

Some of What I Know About Healing

After you've gotten the arrow out
bandaged the broken bone
the real work begins

No one can do it for you
It takes as long as it takes
and usually leaves a scar
It helps to be able to lay down
someplace quiet for a while

especially if there's someone nearby
who will check on you
only as much as you want them to
and also as much as you really need
(for you may feel ashamed of your brokenness)

Sometimes it takes more courage
than you yet own
and there isn't a soul who can learn
to walk again without pain

Sometimes all you can do is accept
the necessary conditions
and trust
that there is wholeness at the heart of things
and you are in the heart of the heart

Even If

There may be a broken wrist
There may be the end to everything

There may be poison oak and pinkeye
and all manner of itchy afflictions

There may be a loss so great
I know not how to envision it

There will be falling
There will be pain
There may come all I fear
and several horrible things I failed to consider

But this I know
this I choose to remember
Despite
amidst
even, unimaginably, *because*
there will be joy

Among the Weary

One day she woke up finished—
done holding the world together
It was falling apart anyway
despite her best efforts
and she decided to wonder
what would happen if
she stopped effing so much

Would the hungry still be hungry?
Would the fed still be fed?
Would the weary find rest?
(And what if she included
herself among the weary?)

Would people stop wanting her?
And what would it mean
if they did—that all along
they had been near for her yield
and not for her self?

She started practicing
a few minutes in the morning
letting go of the handle
she used to crank the world around
Sometimes she opened up her hands
while standing in line
and when everything went on around her
she felt obsolete, useless, unimportant
and below all of that
free

Now she tries to remember
just to stay awake
Now she gives her hands a break
sometimes even in the peak of summer
even at midday

Now she stands to the side
not needing to be at the center
of anyone's life but her own

Andromeda Rising

All these jealous gods
trying to dim their rivals' light

Don't they know what happens
when a star comes under pressure
begins to trust the dark
revolution at her center?

That's how you get galaxies

All the Way to the Center

"I sustained a trauma," I heard her say
and the truth chimed out
into the silence that followed

We never just sustain an injury
It is sustained in us
The pain doesn't stop
when the wreck has come to rest

What could it be
to experience a trauma
but sustain a healing?

What will it take to feel safe enough
to let the tonic penetrate
as deeply as the heartbreak?

Into the Sea

The waves of doubt
are eroding the edges
The tide has receded
and I am feeling whole again
clinging fast to two sure stones

It is easy to want to remain in place
but I know how waves work
Another will come
Old worries with new faces
sweep in and erase
all the lines at the limits
leave me pared and tender

I have grown
just enough
to fit inside this new skin
How many more molting seasons
will I endure here at the brink of the water?
Can I come to welcome
the baring and the baptism?
Perhaps one day I will live with no shell at all
Perhaps one day I will turn into the sea

For Walking Without Certainty

I want to write a blessing for you
to give you a gift
which is also a prayer
a supplication for something beyond
my ability to offer or understand

which is also to say
I am hoping on your behalf
I am hoping for you
for you who stand
with the hands of your heart
cupped and waiting

you the weary
you the joyful
I am thinking of you
right now as I write
while the horns blow in the street below
and the river keeps washing its banks faithfully
like the caretaker dusts the altar rail

But how can I bless you
without either of us cringing
at the way the blessings can be stolen
have been stolen, hoarded, held
(as if there are not always enough to go around)
as if by plastering the word onto our walls
we can ensure we will be one of the chosen few
we who have collected all the lucky tokens
and yet do not have the shiny prizes we were promised

This is not the blessing I have for you today

And too, how many blessings have been carelessly spoken
or heaped up, fortress against fear
or withheld for power
or perhaps for the fear
of the power
of asking for what we want
and walking without certainty

I want to be brave in the blessing
to bless more than is necessary

And so
I give you the blessing of yearning
and of resting in the mystery
the blessing that builds you a shelter
for the journey
and accompanies you
as you make your way
through being human in the world
through becoming whole

See here, this blessing
is in the hand that reaches out to you

See here, this blessing
is the hand that reaches out to you

Fixed Center

I've always felt more kinship with the moon
her radiance changeable and fleeting
retreating and returning like water on sand

But it is the sun which alters
though he appears so steady in the sky
blazing out and roiling with flames too bright to see

And the moon and I, through all our spinning
and every shifting phase
are solid stone

Before and After

It took a lot of work
to come home
into my body and now
as she speaks to me
with the language of emotion
urgently, quietly,
joyfully, anxiously
I find myself wanting at times
to turn my back on her

But I cannot bend away
this spine that is her own
I would have none
without her generosity
nor legs nor nerves
nor hands nor breath

We were once divided
apart from each other
We have fought
sought to become whole
but binding myself so firmly
to this tenuous tender thing
means staying fragile forever
means letting in the dying

It is too much for me today

But what of her?
Does she revel in the life
to which my thoughts admitted her?
Does she not recognize
the danger of being awake?

She sings with electricity
alive alive alive alive
She is animal
with no fear for the ending
no experience of anything but
this heart
beat

I thought I invited her to join me
here in my whirring mind
but she is the now, welcoming me in
into the timeless fleeting

She does not negotiate
not a little bit of feeling
and a little bit of sleep

She is all-in or nothing
and though it pains me
this fear of opening
what will never close again
the portal, once rent
lets in the light
through the open windows of her skin
and she is the only one
with eyes to see it shine

Labor

Most days
the work we are truly called to do
won't feel at all earth shattering

Keep faith and persevere
Who wants a shattered earth anyway?

To Mend Them

Some days I'm tired of the making
but that might be an indication
I'm trying to do it alone
and that's how you end up with armor

Helmets, shields, masks, weapons—
all forged in lonely fires
stoked by the thought of a battle line

That's not how you weave
blankets, tents, or nets
That's not how you make
bigger tablecloths

Still, we live in a world
where the looms have been shattered
and only a few know how to mend them

We have stopped listening to those
who are willing to sit and spin
pulling strength from weakness
plying two and three together

You can't buy a better world on any shelf
The new earth doesn't come ready made
We are always and forever
winding it together from raw materials

Working the Loom

Carried in the center
is the pain of the multitudes
warping the weft of the world

I can't see the pattern yet
but there is around the edges
a shimmering
of the things that want to happen
the way things want to be

Weave the way to wholeness

Repronunciation Guide

Growing up I didn't know
how to say some words correctly
ambulance
nuclear
mischievous
faux

Some I learned by sight not sound
I still hear echoes of old assumptions in my mind
saguaro
photography
raison d'être

The people around me modeled some incorrectly
I will always have to think twice
before I open my mouth
realtor
hors d'oeuvre
February
racial equality

This Time

when the powerless
stood at the crucifixion
they had cameras,
bore witness to the killing
became apostles for the slain

Some of the people
hid in the bunkers
hid behind their shields
hid behind their skin

The women who once
brought spices to the tomb
anointed with milk
the eyes of those
who refused to look away

Working Title

When you're writing a poem
sometimes a line says
almost what wants to be said
but not quite

You're tempted to just leave it
It takes way more work to rewrite it right
than it did to write it wrong in the first place

It takes listening to the lines around the problem
a willingness to let go of the way things are
a lot of wondering how things could be better

But when you get there
to the place that doesn't just make sense for you
but for everyone
you wonder why you ever thought
the status quo was good enough

From the Pile of Papers on the Borrowed Desk

The National Highway Traffic Safety Administration
has issued a bulletin titled
"A guide to your rights and responsibilities for
staying safe as a pedestrian"
and I wish there was a pamphlet like this for everything
A guide to my rights and responsibilities
for staying safe as a human
Someone who could tell me
what I can really expect
and what I really owe
and guarantee my actions could keep me safe

Though I'm afraid I would just use it as an excuse
to be angry if I didn't get what I was promised
and ashamed if anyone pointed out the ways
I was walking against the light
and wandering across the streets cattywampus
And when did "staying safe" become my purpose anyway?

"A public unaware of a problem is unlikely
to be receptive to available solutions" says the subtitle
(the NHTSA not being known for brevity in nomenclature)
but I find myself mostly wishing
for unavailable solutions

Tikkun Olam

As you sit on the sofa
or crosslegged on the bed
and squint over your work
you may not even remember
how to start the stitch
the rhythm of the needle in your hand
the long pull of the thread
and the way the tail
always catches at the twist

It's been so long since
there was time for mending
but you chose a thread
from your memory of color
and it is fading into the work
just as you'd hoped

If you do this well
no one will think twice
of the mender

There is a wholeness to be made
from the remnants
a unity underneath
beyond the rending

Can your old eyes see the weave
the way it wants to fall together?

With tender fingers
piece your material
careful with the edges

Redeliverance

God, did you have to walk gingerly
after giving birth to me?
Had you grown heavy with the weight
of my becoming?
Groan with relief
as I came into the light?
Did my emergence leave you bleeding?
Exhausted?
Ebullient?
What nourishment do you offer me
from your own being?
And what tenderness?

And are you willing to do it again?

Recipe for Manifestation

Have you been at the bottom of despair?
If you don't know, that's okay
I always hedge my measurements of pain
in case it gets worse
and maybe you do, too
But here's what I'm saying
You don't have to know the deepest depths
to need hope, to lose it
to use it up and make some more

Hope isn't optional
You don't buy it with what you earned
when things went wrong
you don't wait for it to show up
like a taxi or a birthday card
Hope is manual labor
You have to choose
to use your hands
to make it manifest
Get right in there and mix up a batch

Psalm Ninety-Six

For all who work to create kerkasiel

We are saved by singing
by listening to one another
Stay, stay with me
Come, throw open the doors

By listening to one another
we step into a sanctuary
As we throw open the doors
our hearts turn toward love

Strangers stepped into a sanctuary
and a circle formed around them
Hearts turned toward love
and the singing never ceased

A circle formed around them
through all the days and nights
and the singing never ceased
The people were in it, praying

Through all the days and nights
this space is only a sanctuary
If the people are in it, praying
and listening, wide with gratitude

This space becomes a sanctuary
as you stay, stay with me
listening, wide with gratitude
We are saved by singing

Not by Sight

We are looking for the way to walk
Some of the ones we had thought we could follow
have already gone away

Perhaps they learned to walk on water
because they left no track
We're beginning to suspect
they may have done this on purpose

Why can it not be just a little easier?
Why not a set of stepping stones left in the mud?
Why not a trail broken through the crust of snow?

We are looking for the way to walk
not yet stepping into the wilderness
No matter how long we wait
there appears no clear course

Here in the dark, viewpoints offer no assistance
This road will not be built by sight
This is how we will live now
by feel, by scent
by the wind on the side of our faces

We are looking for the way to walk
We give up wishing for a path
We lift one foot
begin to set it down when the other lifts too
We were not given steps to follow
We were given wings

Wilderness

Once we had nothing else to do
we started getting creative
and mostly kinder

Sure, there were those
who tried to keep
all the manna for themselves
but it turned to maggots overnight
and we laughed at their bewilderment
though we had secretly
considered doing the same

We worshiped anything golden
because it made us feel powerful
We followed leaders who went in circles
and we wrote new songs to sing on the way

We went for lots of rambles
because someone told us
we could depend on our shoes
Once the old place wasn't an option
it was a long walk together
to somewhere new

The Unpossessing

The day we walked
across the unexplored island
we tore the fruit to bits
trying to locate its taxonomy
disregarding its sweetness

A generation ago or yesterday
we might have named it ourselves
after the one among us
who held the most power
(no matter what it was called
by those who loved it first)

How can I pare away
the piece of me
that thinks I can own
anything but my skin,
my flesh, and my core?

Be Wilder

There are bats in the churches
not in the belfry where one might expect
I'm not even sure we have a belfry anymore
The last one I was in was filled with wasps
and the bells are silent now

No, these bats have stumbled in out of the cold
thinking this place would offer shelter
but now they are calling beyond sound
beyond the reach of heedless ears
They are bumbling about, spreading their wings
crying to be set free

They are trying all the corners, looking for the wilderness
They are dying in the harsh light
They are moving out
through the windows, over the thresholds
They sing their way to open spaces
to where the night is soft and filled with stars
to where the freed ones fly

Come the Glorious Undoing

The Book of Common Prayer
says "We have left undone
those things which we
ought to have done
and we have done those things
which we ought not
to have done"

This is the Morning Prayer of General Confession
a very common prayer indeed
to rue and doubt
one's action and stillness

But what if I have left undone
the very things I would have regretted?
And what if I have chosen
the glorious undoing
the inevitable unavoidable inescapable yes?

It once seemed a decision—
leave home or stay
wander far
return or stay away—
yet from this ridge top
I see a single way
what seems from here to be
the only pass between the peaks

I am only psychic in hindsight
cartographer of memory
sketching the voyage
so simply in reflection
excusing unvisited continents
with the fear of dragons

Yet how can I lament this course
if I am led again and after that again
always back into my eggshell skin?

It is not too late to send the spirit wandering
to leap and trust the wind to catch and carry
It is never too late to learn the dragon's names

Love

Love isn't the final exam
You can't cram it in at the end

Don't you want to have been
passing it out
indiscriminately
all along?

Written on the Side of the Road, Nearly Weeping

He was only giving me my receipt
his gas-stained hands
reaching through my window
with a slip of paper
I promptly discarded
in the trash bag on the floor
But I had heard him breathe
a deep, sad sigh
as he walked up to the pump
to perform the benediction
And so I said
I hope you have a good day
like I really meant it
because I really did
I saw the look in his eyes
when his heart
caught the truth
my heart was saying
underneath

You matter
You are beloved
I love you
I
Love
You

I could feel the shutters
fall closed on my face
as I looked away first
started the car
and drove off from the cathedral

because people with propriety
don't let their soul show
in public
It is not socially acceptable
to love this much
even especially the ones who need it most

And I am often afraid
of the fire I would ignite
if I let the flint strike

Love has spilled out
all over this world
The fumes of love are heavy in the air
If I look, I can see it shimmer

Every day
be a falling spark
Shut off the sprinklers
Hide the hoses
Let it burn

Good Practice

He says I could go to a silent retreat
and come home with a new friend
that I could find them, be found by them
at stoplights, in drive-throughs
in checkout lines, in traffic jams
But right now I can't go any of those places
I miss meeting strangers
deciding right away I'm going to love them

Maybe that's why I've started greeting
every new bloom on our walks
We took bets for a while on what color
the tulips would turn out to be
shook hands with the rosemary
welcomed the irises
as if we hadn't seen them for a year

I don't have to waste time
secretly hoping
these new friends will like me
I just get to adore them
as long as they live
notice the way they blossom
uniquely, completely
yearn for them when they are gone

Special Delivery

Tassels hang potent from filbert trees
The sun pulls a cloud bandanna over her face

Daffodils beam from country ditches
Pollen motes drift into magnolia's cupped fingertips
Yellow has been declared the color of the season

The starling has moved into the corner office above the porch
Is calling through the keyhole to summon the stenographer

Spring is sending you a love letter

From This Day

They veered from the well-worn path
skirted the half-wall
and walked through the waiting room
near my seat behind the harp

Perhaps they took the off-ramp
because even the slow lane was too fast
for his unsteady feet

She matched her stride to his
and they took their time
a few more moments to savor
the music rising slow

I glanced up from the strings
Was that a bit of a shimmy?
An aged shuffle or a seasoned cha cha?
I'd like to think she's dancing

They have been living their vows
every day for a long time now
making and keeping their everyday promises
So something in the set of his shoulders
makes me wonder
did they take the long way around
to walk an aisle again today?

Here on the first floor, near the elevator
it would be easy to assume today's troth
is for sickness
for poorer
for worse

But there—she is reaching
for his hand
He is reaching back
This could be the better

Hush

Behind the mask of words
you are begging to be seen
I can see this

The air is too full for me to see
you

Still
be still
for just a moment
I will keep looking

Safe Enough to Brave

When I wake in the night and the terror
that daylight keeps at bay
has crept out of the closet
and is standing by the bed
its face filling my vision
until there is nothing else to see
until there will never
be anything else to be
but frightened and alone

I become a hammock
swinging on a summer day
I become the ropes holding on
Heels and hair anchor me deep
and the threads weave under and in me
from the love of those who come to mind
Some are fragile but I am held

I lie in the web of the hearts I trust
Cocooned in the fabric of the ones
who make it safe enough to brave
my own life again

If I could, I would spin a skein
for each of you
bring it over on a sunny afternoon
and tell you how
to save it for a dark night

You can put it in the closet
next to the shoes you never wear
and all the nocturnal visitors
It will be there for you
even to the end
even if you are in pain
even if you appear to be alone
It will wind over and around you with mercy
It will carry you all the way home

Instructions for Today

(and/or for the apocalypse)

Go slowly
Stay simple
Draw near to all you love
Love all who are nearby
Take care of each other
Resist fear
Resist violence
Walk hand in hand
even if you walk together to the end

What Awaits

Death isn't the last thing on my bucket list
I have all sorts of intentions for eternity

If I don't get around to it here
I plan to learn to play the cello
to become a half-assed tennis player
nap for a millennium or two

I might dabble in photography
and several thousand burbling creeks

I intend to stare at the moon
in each of her phases
from a hilltop on every planet
a moon calls home
(I will need a few decades on Jupiter alone)

I want to spend a lifetime
getting to know you
every single one of you
Take a century or two apiece
to practice loving each other well
until we really get it down

But no matter what awaits
an eternity spent held in the warmth of belonging
a return to the womb of the source of love
a reincarnation as a giraffe
or a scorpion or fruit fly or truffle pig
or a new life more like this one
with cherry trees and Earl Grey
and glaciers and coastlines and curiosity

I hope somehow, past the great curtain of mystery
as the overture ends and the play begins
I hope there is a pen
a quiet place and a blank page
I hope I get to write about it

All the Way From Spring to Salt

For their final exam
river pilots must draw
the entire channel from memory

I may never know anything
this completely
        not my lover
             who charts his own way
        the mother I've sketched
with a thousand lines
        nor my children either

        It was clear from the first
the moment each cast off
        from their own private sea
     and I have long since settled into
        a near constant state of surprise
at confluences I cannot fathom

Bar pilots will have made
one hundred independent crossings
before being declared accomplished

        My body has almost forgotten
            the place we once were joined
        I am an oxbow now

You don't like pancakes for breakfast anymore
Green is your new favorite color
The names I gave you no longer serve

     I hold the lead line coiled at hand
        drop it daily from the bow
            draw it up and mark new depths

Skilled navigators trust today's observations
more than yesterday's measurements
for the sands are always shifting

        No map exists that can
        carry you to safety

    I surrender to the drifting flow
loving even the rapids
        as you cut your own banks deeper

You spread out to inhabit
                your entire floodplain

    You rise with the force of the sea
      as the ocean ebbs upstream

        You gather every drop of snowmelt
to scour away all that no longer belongs
            at your side

See Through

I.
Why not all the love you can offer?
Why not all the beauty you can hold?

II.
There's a window, she said
that only you can see
Outside is a night sky
stars and a moon
No, sometimes it's the night
but it always changes
so you have to keep looking
you have to keep telling
what is out the window
Because if we believe it
believe there is a way to see
beyond this dark passage
we might be able to notice
we might all begin to see
how each one of us can be
standing near a window
singing in the mystery

Who would ever say to the maple tree
"You are not doing enough to save the world"?
Or speak to the trillium, saying
"Your life is too fragile to matter"?

With roots both deep and wide
each holds the earth together
with the force of being what they are
with the power of being whole

Etude for Belonging

You belong

yes, you, who are reading these words with doubt
whose lips are already forming
the shape of an argument

Rest

You belong in your body
this body
not just the portion of it
you find acceptable

You belong in your body
and your body belongs

Rest

You belong in your mind
sweet mind, held always by what was
fearful of what will be
afraid of the astonishment of yes

You belong in your mind
and your mind belongs

Rest

You belong in your spirit
beautiful slash in the skin of the source
where a flicker of light pours through
universal and unique

You belong in your spirit
and your spirit belongs

Rest

Roots, cliffs, migration paths
all these hold our kindred sure
Are we the only beings
who wonder about our place?

Rest

How long can you suspend your disbelief
and trust the warp and weft
beyond the gravity of space and time
that cradles your radiance?

Practice belonging

How long can you hold yourself
and let yourself be held
in the embrace of this moment?

Rest

This is not a counting song
where the beats tick past ascending

One
Two
Three
Four

Love is a long sustain
Let us measure our belonging together

One
One
One
One

When Something New Is on the Way

In the last hour before giving birth
when pain blazed high
and shadowed everything
beyond its brilliant flare
I couldn't remember why
I was giving my life away

I lost hold of all I thought I could keep
lost all hope for what was to be
The knowing of what I had come to do
turned to ashes on the fading embers
The one within me remembered
The one within me remembers

To Help You Remember Why

What does it cost to fall
in love with the world?

To find yourself
knocked out with fondness
over each one's face
and astonishing gifts
with this forget-me-not
and every beating heart?

It's not a safe way to live
in love with everything
for all of it is dying
Every one of us
and every blossom falls
before the soul is ready

Take courage, stay open, be tender
Be brave, dear heart, be brave

Confession

I'm not sure I should tell you
that I'm still afraid to die
and worse, afraid to live through
all the loss I know is coming

I have been a young and joyful being
and I live in the shade
of the old and joyful ones
but I don't know how to walk
from one to the other
on this path of fallen leaves

Even if this is not the age
in which we slaughter our planet
they say the frogs will never be the same

I can't decide if I might as well go then
after all the orcas have drowned
The flowers have already begun to wilt
and petals are dropping faster than ever
one by one and, sometimes
all at once
but, oh, the beauty remaining
on the barren branches

There will never be enough time
to love as each deserves
and I think some who feel this most deeply
determine not to love at all
never begin so as never to fail

I choose to be a glorious disaster
to die with the work of love undone

For Miracles and Incarnation

They advise the parents and teachers
not to say "Don't"
to the small ones among us
"Children learn better when we say 'yes'
when we speak what it is
we want them to be"

So instead of "Don't take off your shoes"
or "Don't get out of bed again"
we speak in awkward communal positives
"We're going to keep our shoes on right now"
"It's time for us to have a rest"

No one taught this to the angels
who come, each one
wings flared, eyes blazing
shouting to the cowering mortals
"Do not be afraid!"

For we all are sore afraid
of war and uncertainty
landslides and the death of bees
of rising tides and broken legs
and bombs and often of each other

And yet the practice of turning
to face what we cannot understand
is the very thing that makes room
for miracles and incarnation

I say to the small ones among us
to you and to the fright in me
"Yes," I say, "and yes and yes"
I speak what it is we want to be

"We will not be afraid right now
It is time for us to take courage"

Coda

Before a beginning
practice the ending
the last note ringing out
and the silence after

Practice the corpse pose
still mind resting in love
As it was in the beginning
it will be in the end

Let every chord sing fearlessly
to its completion
Let it decay

Practice the nightfall
which holds the dawn
within its tinted palm

Receive winter's darkest day
solstice swinging up to spring

Allow your heart
every small surrender
the broken cup
the fallen fruit

Let this come to close
and this
with joy in the releasing

Then, still
begin

Title Index

First Line Index

W

Y

9 781594 980756